DOLPHINS

A Photo Book of Ocean Facts for Curious Kids

The Natural World Library

BRIGHT HABITAT PRESS

Dolphins

A Photo Book of Ocean Facts for Curious Kids

Printed in the United States of America
ISBN-13: 979-8-88700-628-4 | Paperback

About This Book

Dolphins introduces young readers to one of the ocean's most intelligent and playful animals through real photographs and simple facts.

Each page pairs a clear image with easy-to-understand information that helps children learn how dolphins live, move, communicate, and survive in the ocean. The facts are written for early learners and designed to encourage curiosity, observation, and discussion.

This book is part of The Natural World Library from Bright Habitat Press, a series created to help children explore animals and habitats through real images and age-appropriate science.

Dolphins are marine mammals that live in oceans around the world.

Dolphins breathe air through a blowhole on top of their heads.

Dolphins have smooth bodies that help them swim fast.

Dolphins use their tails, called flukes, to move through the water.

Dolphins have fins that help them steer and stay balanced.

Dolphins are strong swimmers and can leap out of the water.

Dolphins can swim long distances without getting tired.

Dolphins eat fish and other sea animals.

Dolphins use echolocation to find food underwater.

Echolocation helps dolphins understand their surroundings.

Dolphins often swim together in groups called pods.

Dolphins work together to help one another find food.

Dolphins are playful and curious animals.

Baby dolphins are called calves.

Dolphin calves stay close to their mothers.

Mother dolphins help calves learn.

Dolphins make clicks and whistles to communicate.

Dolphins use sounds and body movements to share information.

Dolphins live in warm and cool oceans worldwide.

Some dolphins live near coasts, others in open ocean.

Dolphins help keep ocean ecosystems healthy.

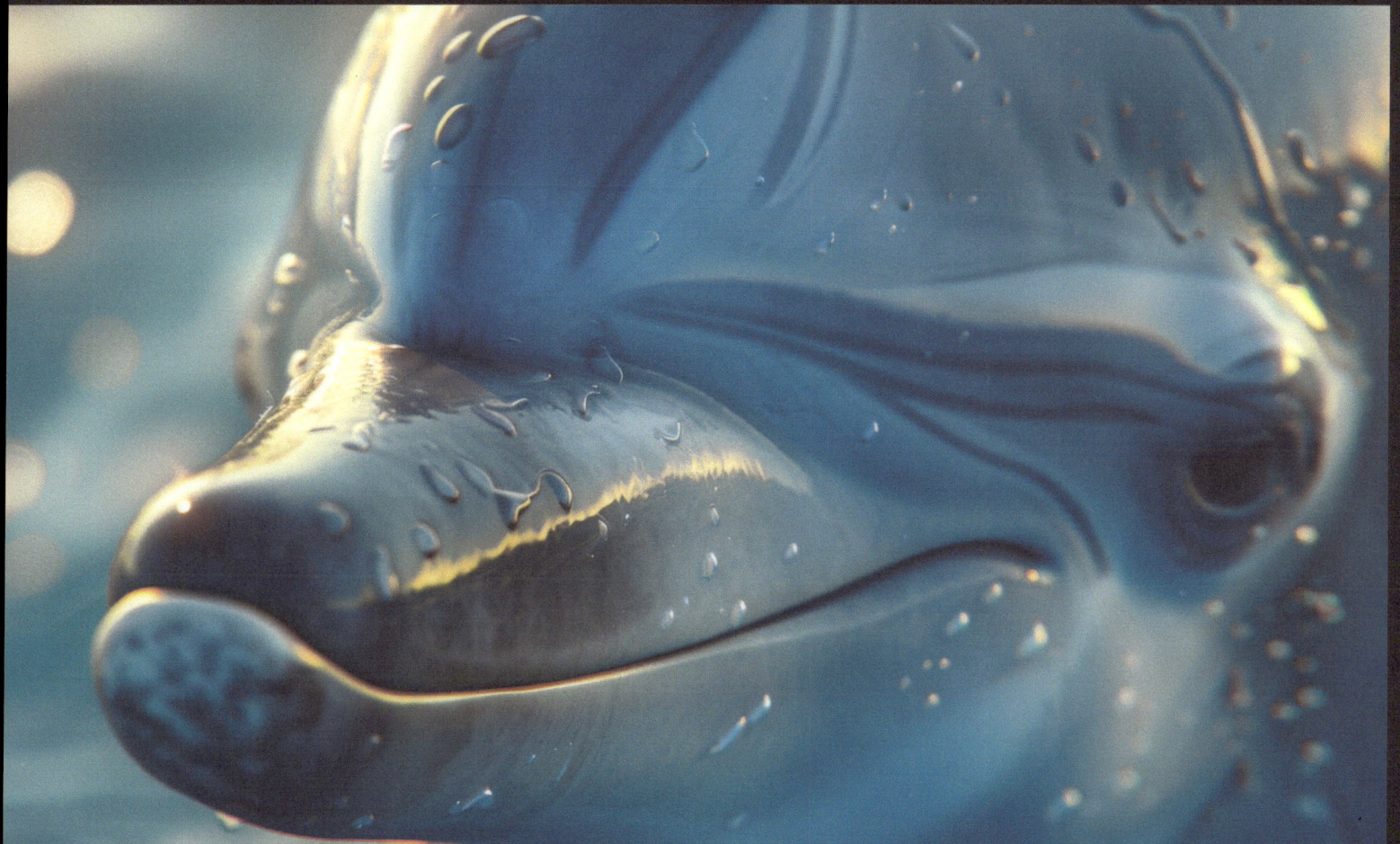

Dolphins help scientists learn about oceans.

Dolphins have lived in oceans for millions of years.

Dolphins are protected in many parts of the world.

Bright Habitat Press creates educational picture books that help children explore animals, nature, and the world around them through real photographs and clear facts.

Our books are designed to support early learning and curiosity in young readers.

www.ingramcontent.com/pod-product-compliance
Lightning Source LLC
Chambersburg PA
CBHW060855270326

41934CB00002B/145